successful
self-motivation

Frances Coombes

...iries: please contact Bookpoint Ltd,
...Abingdon, Oxon OX14 4SB.
...+44 (0) 1235 827720. *Fax:* +44 (0) 1235 400454.
Lines are open 09.00–17.00, Monday to Saturday, with a 24-hour message answering service. Details about our titles and how to order are available at www.hoddereducation.com

British Library Cataloguing in Publication Data: a catalogue record for this title is available from the British Library.

First published in UK 2011 by Hodder Education, part of Hachette UK, 338 Euston Road, London NW1 3BH.

Copyright © 2011 Frances Coombes

In UK: All rights reserved. Apart from any permitted use under UK copyright law, no part of this publication may be reproduced or transmitted in any form or by any means, electronic or mechanical, including photocopy, recording, or any information, storage and retrieval system, without permission in writing from the publisher or under licence from the Copyright Licensing Agency Limited. Further details of such licences (for reprographic reproduction) may be obtained from the Copyright Licensing Agency Limited, of Saffron House, 6–10 Kirby Street, London EC1N 8TS.

Typeset by MPS Limited, a Macmillan Company.

Printed in Great Britain for Hodder Education, an Hachette UK Company, 338 Euston Road, London NW1 3BH, by CPI Cox & Wyman, Reading, Berkshire RG1 8EX.

The publisher has used its best endeavours to ensure that the URLs for external websites referred to in this book are correct and active at the time of going to press. However, the publisher and the author have no responsibility for the websites and can make no guarantee that a site will remain live or that the content will remain relevant, decent or appropriate.

Hachette UK's policy is to use papers that are natural, renewable and recyclable products and made from wood grown in sustainable forests. The logging and manufacturing processes are expected to conform to the environmental regulations of the country of origin.

Impression number   10 9 8 7 6 5 4 3 2 1
Year   2015 2014 2013 2012 2011

London Borough of Enfield	
91200000049222	
Askews & Holts	Apr-2011
153.8	£5.99

Contents

1	What is motivation?	2
2	Motivation at work	10
3	Create a compelling future	16
4	Incentives to produce good ideas	26
5	Sharpen your thinking	36
6	The power of setting goals	46
7	Take control of how you think	56
8	Model success strategies	64
9	Pick a skill you want to acquire	74
10	Coaching your inner team	82
11	Model success to master change	86

what is motivation?

How good are you at motivating yourself to get things done? Do you have areas you would like to change or improve your levels of motivation in? We can all benefit from learning more effective means to achieve our goals in life.

Motivation is an inner drive, an energy within us that gives us the ability to act; it propels us towards reaching our ultimate aims. When a person is motivated they achieve more of the things they want to do; they are successful.

Motivation works best within a framework of setting goals, planning and taking actions. Being motivated, and planning without taking action is futile. Being motivated, and taking action without planning ahead is fatal. Miss out any of these steps and you miss your chance of succeeding.

The trick is to set the right goals, in the right chunk sizes and order, so that ultimately you can achieve anything you want in life.

What is motivation?

> *'Whatever you do, or dream you can, begin it. Boldness has genius and power and magic in it.'*
>
> Goethe 1747–1832

Motivation is a state of mind, an attitude, a way of thinking, being and doing that can reap rewards beyond your wildest dreams. Just as preparing for a team sport or getting ready for a first date requires you to think tactically and become aware of how other players may engage, becoming highly motivated requires that you develop new skills and a new sense of awareness that wasn't necessary in your less ambitious state.

How motivated are you?

> *'Success is not the result of spontaneous combustion. You must set yourself on fire.'*
>
> Reggie Leach

* What are the things that you are naturally drawn to?
* What are the changes you will need to make to get the life you want?

When you know what you want in life, and can recognize the environment, behaviour, lack of skills or resources, or limiting beliefs that may be holding you back you can begin to solve problems that might be preventing you from achieving your full success potential. One way to do this is to ask yourself lots of questions out loud. Human beings have evolved by solving puzzles; they are problem-seeking missiles, designed to home in and find answers once a question has been voiced.

How motivated are you?

How motivated are you to achieve the things that are really important to you in life? Do you identify with any of the methods below that people employ to achieve their aims in life? On a motivation scale of 1–10, where do you fit? Write your answer in column 2.

Wish list You wish you had achieved your goal, but nothing happens and you wonder why.	
Want it You want your outcome and you start out to achieve it, but when things don't go your way you give up frustrated.	
Want it, sometimes get it, often don't When you do give up it is because you realize halfway through that the price is too high.	
Want it, envision and plan your route You achieve your goal, celebrate, move on to a new target and expect to get that too.	

Being motivated is the nearest thing to magic you can achieve because it develops a 'can do' attitude, which is the most critical accessory to success in any endeavour. Anyone who is totally motivated and achieving his or her goals on a regular basis may find it hard to understand the person who settles for dawdling through life and accepting whatever fate, or the result of their inaction, chooses to deal them. So let's start thinking about changes you want to make.

What do you want?

A well-formed outcome is your personal map towards your goal. It is a framework used to help you define clear and achievable results. If you start out with your own unique map of how to proceed at any point along your route, you will wildly increase your chances of success.

Use positive outcome thinking

When you set a goal, it is important to clarify exactly what you want. It is equally important to know what achieving your goal will give you that you don't have now. It is also vital to know what evidence of success you will need to see to convince yourself that you have achieved your aim.

Apply the question strategy

How will you know you have got your goal? When you have a goal, for example 'I want to be rich', the questions to ask to ascertain how you will know when you have achieved your goal are:

Q How will you know you are rich?
A Because I won't have to work.
Q And what will you see, hear and feel when you've got what you want?
A I will see myself sitting in a lovely apartment by the beach. I will feel free and easy and contented as I hear my family playing in the pool.

You can continue the questions above by asking: 'And what else will let you know …?', 'What else will you see, hear and feel?' The more vividly a goal is imagined, the more the unconscious mind will strive to achieve it.

Preparing a well-formed outcome

By modelling the steps that most successful people follow when setting their outcomes, you will increase your chances of achieving your goals. Besides asking the questions above, 'What do I want?' and 'What will I see, hear and feel to let me know I have achieved my goal?', other questions to consider are:

* Where do I want my outcome (at home/at work)?
* How will me achieving my outcome affect my workmates, my family, my friends?

Think about the impact of you initiating this new goal and how you would deal with any difficulties that might arise. What are the costs and benefits of achieving the goal? What will you gain from achieving your aim? What do you get from what you are doing at present? Is there anything you might lose by achieving your outcome?

How much control do you have over your outcome?

You will probably never have complete control over any situation where other people or finances or market changes are involved, but the more influence you can have over the outcome, the more likely you are to be able to achieve it.

What resources do you bring to the undertaking?

* Skills?
* Knowledge?
* Information?
* Time?
* Money?
* Connections?

Do you have any or all of the resources you need, or know how to get them? For instance, you may not have the money, or all of the knowledge, but do you know someone who does? Could you barter with them for their input if it helps to increase your chances of success?

* What is a realistic timeframe to set for your goal?
* What will you do about anything that may get in the way?

What would achieving your goal say about you?

* If you achieve your goal, what else will you get?
* What is this goal a step towards?
* What is the next step in achieving your goal?
* Do you still want your goal?

By framing your goals in a well-formed outcome you give yourself the greatest chance of achieving them. The process also helps you to clarify whether or not you really want the outcome before you set out on the undertaking. By thinking the situation through you will have saved yourself time, possibly money, and effort, which you can use to focus on the things you really burn to achieve.

What is the most important thing I can do?

One of the most powerful questions anyone who wants to start achieving can ask themselves each day is, 'What are the most important things I can do today to take me nearer to my goals?' Then, and this is important, **they follow through with actions**. Initially it might be:
* a telephone call to find out more about something
* looking for books or ideas about someone who's done similar things
* a plan of action
* sorting out your skills and abilities
* attending seminars and workshops
* finding and talking to people who share your dreams
* looking for the next step to take that leads towards your goals.

An idea is only a notion – unless an action follows.

What things do you regret not having done?

A magazine survey of people in their eighties, which asked the question 'If you had your life over again, what would you do differently?', reveals that the majority of people said:
* I would focus more on my values and larger goals and not be driven by day-to-day decisions.
* I would have more courage in taking risks in my career and relationships.
* I would leave a legacy, do more things for other people.

How do you know if you really want your goal?

Imagine an outcome you really desire. What are you 'seeing' and saying to yourself? Describe the emotions you feel. Now imagine not pursuing your goal. The feeling you have now is the difference you will feel between pursuing your goal or shutting down on that desire. Do you still want your goal?

motivation at work

'Most people are only five or six skills away from achieving the successes they want in life,' said Robert Kiyosaki, author of the multi-million-pound New York best seller, *Rich Dad, Poor Dad*. Which six strategies could you acquire to generate powerful leverage in the areas you seek to excel in? It may be:

Better communication skills at work, or to build rapport with others.

To get your message across to customers, negotiate or listen with greater insight and clarity.

To discover how another person weighs up a situation in order to make a decision.

To anchor a confident state when you may not feel that way.

To create the life you want combine motivation with tactical thinking and doing, and use simple strategies like the above that are aligned towards you goals. Start designing and using your own software for your brain.

Align your values with the work you do

The secret of living a meaningful life is to know who you are, and what your values are. Combine this with knowing where you are going in life and have a written blueprint for how you will get there.

Values are the principles which drive our behaviour; they give meaning to our lives. When we engage in what we do with our values then we engage in projects with our hearts and minds.

Bring your heart to work

Identify what's important to you, using values

Start thinking about the things you value most. Use this list to prompt you and add your own values to it.

achievement	fun	justice	security
adventure	growth	kindness	self-discipline
beauty	happiness	knowledge	self-esteem
charity	health	leadership	service
community	honesty	love	spirituality
creativity	honour	peace	strength
dignity	humility	power	supportiveness
ethics	independence	pride	surrender
family	individuality	reason	trust
freedom	integrity	respect	truth
friendship	intimacy	risk	wisdom

Pick ten values which are most important to you. Beside each one write the reason why this quality is important to you. You might write:

Creativity *Creativity is important to me because ... it lets me express myself.*

Freedom *Freedom is important to me because ... I want the freedom to decide what I do.*

Follow your values to increase motivation

Once you know what your values are the next thing to find out is what actions associated with those values would make you feel you were achieving your life's purpose.

Motivation and peak performance

Motivation and peak performance come from knowing what you want to achieve in life. Many of us move through life with a few goals and objectives but without a real sense of purpose. Our goals are often more about what we don't want rather than moving towards the things we do want. We might say we want a better job, partner, or home, but our main wish is to get away from our current situation.

Assumptions to adopt for peak performance

Positive assumption	Reason
If what you are doing is not working, do something else.	If you do what you have always done, you will get what you have always got.
There is no failure, only feedback. What really matters is that you learn from the results.	Whatever occurs, you can use the feedback to change your future behaviour and improve your results.
People have all the resources they need to make changes that will make a difference to their performance.	You already know the answer. There is always something you can do to make a difference and the answer is usually an inner resource.
We all have different versions and viewpoints about how we view reality. To build rapport with someone, join them in their world.	We filter information about the world through our senses and each person focuses on different aspects and creates different models of reality.
You cannot change another person, you can only change yourself.	Changing your behaviour will change other people's responses to you.
Visualizing and thinking about the changes you want to make is the first step to making improvements in your life.	Changes start off as thoughts, they are structured and communicated in pictures and words and become actions.

Mental rehearsal trains the mind

Mental rehearsal prepares you for events and trains your unconscious mind to perform tasks in a predetermined way. Most physical tasks, such as breathing, walking, driving a car, are carried out unconsciously, once the initial preparation work of learning has been done. By mentally rehearsing future successful outcomes you are communicating with your mind through pictures, inner dialogue, feelings, tastes and smells, and building up patterns about how events will play out.

Take responsibility for making things happen

With peak performance comes taking responsibility for making things happen. It involves living your life by creating your future stance rather than drifting through life and reacting to situations that happen to you. People who have high levels of personal mastery continually expand their ability to create the results in life they want to achieve.

Take a course in personal mastery

Reflect upon how much of what you do is based on randomness? How much of what you do is done on purpose? How often do you hear yourself say 'the opportunity came up so I took it'?

* Do you set objectives in isolation that are unconnected to any other goals?
* Do you set objectives that are based on living your purpose?
* Are all of your goals in alignment and are they moving towards your purpose?

> To show commitment, you should take an action that leads towards your goal within 24 hours of setting it.

You have the power to change your thinking

You have the power to change your thinking at will. You can change your thoughts now in order to achieve the feelings you want to have when you have achieved your goal. The idea is to bring those feelings from the future forwards so you are feeling them right now, before you have achieved your success.

Feel good, before you achieve your outcome

Think about a particular goal you want to achieve. It might be 'I want to become the best person that anyone could choose to hire in my particular area of expertise.'

Now imagine that you already are that person: feel it, see it, hear it.

* What are the extra qualities you, as your successful future self, possess that may not have been present before?
* What extra skills have you acquired, and why?
* Write down three main new beliefs you are holding about your future self and your abilities that make you feel happy and assured of your future success.

3

create a compelling future

The greatest gift you can give yourself is to allow yourself to dream. The actress Whoopi Goldberg had no screen role models to copy when, as a child, she imagined herself a movie actress. From an early age she visualized herself being a successful movie star. She stayed constant to her dream and lived it in reality.

What you see repeatedly in your mind's eye is what you tend to achieve. If you see yourself as successful, then you become it. Believing that something can be done sets the wheels in motion to find a way to achieve it.

However, imagination is not a substitute for action but a supplement to it. You can visualize yourself being a pop star or a world-class athlete, yet unless you also take the follow-through actions towards it, nothing much is going to happen. The secret is in imagining – dream it, then do it.

'Dream it – then do it!' This may sound simplistic, but that is exactly how we determine our level of achievement. We imagine vividly the things we want to achieve and then take the actions that propel us towards our goals.

Your level of motivation is the key to success in every area of your life. The more frequently you see yourself achieving the things you aim for, the more likely you are to achieve them and to picture yourself as a winner.

Your success depends upon:

* the things you choose to focus on in life
* the meaning or interpretation you put upon the information you receive
* the action you take as a result of processing that information.

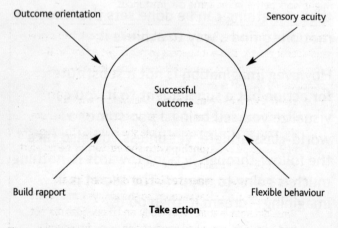

Figure 4.1 *Six habits that lead to success.*

> **Principles for Success Model, taken from neuro-linguistic programming (NLP)**
> * Start with the end in mind. Always know what you want.
> * Build good relationships with people and yourself.
> * Be flexible and generate lots of different types of behaviours until you get the responses you want.
> * Notice when you get the responses you want.
>
> If you adopt this behaviour you will achieve the things you want.

How to use constructive feedback

Using these operating principles of NLP will give you constant feedback on your behaviour, and whether what you are doing is achieving the results you want. Take note of all feedback you receive and ask yourself how you can improve your performance and avoid any unwanted happenings next time. Isolate the behaviour or actions you took that did not serve your purpose, and plan what might work better in the same circumstances.

> Joan Cross, a freelance feature writer, wanted to break into a new newspaper market. She put up ideas to her target editor on the phone and then listened to the response. Using the operating principles for success she:
> * **started with her aim in mind.** She went in with the intention of selling her ideas, had an outline of the feature, the slant and the names of people she intended to interview.
> * **built a good relationship with the editor,** by being alert, attentive and sticking to the point.
> * **was flexible and generated lots of different ideas.** Editors live in an ideas vacuum, so she always had at least three different feature ideas ready, and if one idea did not find favour, then she had another one ready for editorial consideration. She was ready to change the article to take account of the editor's ideas for how a feature should look, and to change interviewees depending on the editor's choices.

* **noticed when she achieved the responses she wanted.** Over a couple of phone calls she began to recognize how the editor preferred to be approached. She achieved several commissions by: noticing that the editor liked her to comment on or praise some aspect of the newspaper section's content; stating when she would get back in touch with the editor; stating who she would use for case studies. In order to remember, Joan wrote down the criteria for achieving good results and consulted it before making each phone call.

Believe that what you want is possible

Define exactly what works for you and do more of it. Keep a record of the behaviour that serves you well and use it as a template for future success.

Notice small details in your own and other people's behaviour. It is not enough for someone to say 'I know I can do that'; always ask, 'How do you know you can do that? What are you seeing, feeling, saying to yourself that lets you know you can do it?' Build up a sense of the events and sequences people need to imagine, feel and hear in order to know whether they can or cannot do something. If you know exactly how someone else does something excellently that you would like to do, you can take that knowledge and model their behaviour so you get the same results.

Visualize to create a compelling future

Visualization is the act of creating compelling and vivid pictures in your mind. When we constantly visualize achieving our goals:
* we focus on our outcome and our brain becomes attuned to notice available resources
* we attract others to us, who bring the opportunities and resources we need to achieve our goals
* we enhance our performance.

We dream about the things we want to achieve and then take the necessary actions that propel us towards our goals. The more frequently you see yourself achieving your goals the more likely you are to achieve them and to see yourself as a winner.

Being successful at reaching your goals is the biggest and most important gift you can give yourself. By increasing your imaginative abilities to build strong visual images of whatever you want to achieve, you are more likely to get it.

Anchor a positive state

Most people can associate with different states and feelings at will. All it takes to trigger their mental movie is to say to them, 'remember when ... we went to the party/stayed out all night/got lost on the way to cousin Delia's wedding?' and they will do the rest themselves.

Notice how people's eyes will fix on a spot where they see the events happening? It is as if they are in a trance. Their shoulders will crumple, their breathing slows down as they relive the emotions they felt that first time. You can choose a ritual like this for you, linked to success. Use it as a trigger to recall a time when you felt truly alive and powerful, when everything you did seemed like magic.

* Think of a personal moment of success that you have experienced and vividly run through the events several times in your mind.
* Associate with those feelings and notice what you see. Are there events happening which bring those pictures near? Notice what you feel; are you excited, buzzing, on a high? What does it feel like for you? What can you hear going on around you? Are people talking or listening?
* When you feel at the height of your experience freeze-frame a mental snapshot of what is going on.
* Use a signal, such as pressing your middle finger and thumb together as a trigger to anchor that feeling at its height of intensity, so that you can recall the picture at will whenever you want to, and get the good feeling when you touch your fingers together.

In the future, by repeating the finger pressing action, you will be able to summon up your successful state, picture and feelings at any time you want to feel powerful, successful and in control.

Successful people, regardless of their areas of achievement, have patterns of motivation and behaviour which they display in order to reach their aim.

* They decide what they want to accomplish.
* They focus on its attainment, and visualize the possession, recognition and acclaim they will receive, and how they will feel when they have realized their dream.
* They believe that the outcome they want to achieve is possible.
* They take the actions necessary to reach their goal.

Generate good ideas

Good ideas don't just come to a few gifted people: they are free to anyone who is prepared to put their minds to work and imagine how they will create their dreams. They will calculate their odds of winning at whatever they want to achieve and the type of skills and talents that they will require to reach their goal, and who they will need to help them on their way. The bigger the dream the more likely it is that they will need to inspire other people to help them reach their target.

Build a shared dream

Successful people in many fields use imaging. Effective leaders in industry, sport, politics and anywhere where team effort is required seek to influence their teams by their actions and words. To motivate others successfully they need to have energy and a good image of themselves as winners, and to convey the excitement and challenge of what they are doing to engage their workforce, the foot soldiers responsible for making success happen.

Motivators often define their aims by using a shared vision or metaphor of what it looks or feels like while they are engaging in the activity that makes them successful. This shorthand description of how their leader sees success enables team members to recognize instantly what it feels like when they are acting effectively in pursuit of team goals.

Look for the metaphors in language

Metaphors are words and stories that people use to describe the way things are, and how they view the world. To know how people view a situation and organize their lives listen to the metaphors they attach to what they are describing. Metaphors contain the structure of how we view our obstacles and desires.

What is your metaphor for work or life?

Look for the metaphors – the descriptive words – that people use to see how they view situations because this will tell you what their inner world looks like:

* 'It's a piece of cake' – they think something is easy to do.
* 'It's a minefield' – they see the situation as dangerous and believe that unexpected difficulties are likely to arise.
* 'With a good wind behind us' – provided there are no unexpected happenings they feel they are likely to achieve their aims.
* 'I feel blocked' or, 'hemmed in' – they feel there are almost physical objects standing in the way of what they want to do.
* 'I feel on top of the world' – they feel really great, as if they are standing on top of the situation.
* 'I can't get around it/over it/under it/through it' – these descriptions all illustrate that they feel there to be a block or barrier between where they are now and whatever they want to achieve.

Metaphors of success

If you want a snapshot of how a person sees the world, listen for the little personal metaphors they include when they describe an action, an event or the world as being like something else. This tells you what things feel like to them.

If you said life is like a 'battlefield' then we might assume that you see continual conflict in your life. People give all sorts of descriptions for this, some see their world as being 'orchestrated by a conductor', 'one long holiday', 'a nightmare', 'like a roller coaster' or 'full of wonder'. These people could all be sharing the same office but still have completely different ways of interpreting the incoming information they receive from their surroundings, based on how their individual models of the world work.

Creating good ideas

Before you can make your visions a reality, you have to create some good ideas that align with the sorts of things that others want and which are currently in demand. We create our ideas by thinking about what often seem like problems and imagining how we might resolve them. Solutions usually come after people have done the necessary preparation and have gathered information around the subject.

Imagine it, then do it

Believing that something can be done sets the wheels in motion to find a way to achieve it. Until Roger Bannister ran the four-minute mile in 1954 nobody believed a human being could possibly run so fast; it was believed to be medically unsafe. In the same year that Bannister achieved his dream, 30 other athletes broke the four-minute mile record – simply because they now had evidence and believed that it could be done. Our beliefs, which are not necessarily reality, determine what we can and cannot do.

Do you have dreams that you would like to achieve that you presently think are impossible? Why not allow yourself some time to dream about them? Is it worth spending ten minutes to examine whether some of the things you secretly desire might just be achievable? After all, you have nothing to lose.

Action

Think of something special you would really like to achieve, but feel you can't. Write it down. Suspend judgement of yourself and your capabilities and spend ten minutes of completely uncensored fun just listing all the reasons why you know that you are the person to do this thing.

Changing beliefs from can't to can

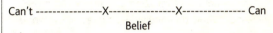

* If you have a skill even remotely linked to what you want to do – maybe one that could be developed – write it down.
* If you are in a unique position to have knowledge about this thing, say, because it's in your workplace, write it down.
* If you believe that you could achieve your aim if only you believed more strongly, write it down.
* If you know what would have to happen to convince yourself you could do it – write it down.
* If you know people who could help you, it doesn't matter whether you think they would or not, write it down.
* If you know some or all of the steps you would have to take to achieve your goal, write them down.

Has your thinking changed about reaching that goal? Do you feel in any way that your outcome might be closer and more possible now? Sometimes people who do this exercise come up with an idea completely different from the one they originally thought of.

4
incentives to produce good ideas

There are at least five stages to being imaginative and producing good ideas, although some people have many more.

First you see the problem, need, aim or goal – you want to achieve something and you think about what you would like to do.

You investigate all the possibilities you can for developing the idea. You look at what went before, what might work, and you imagine combinations of ideas to see what you can come up with.

Then comes the incubation period where you put your subconscious to work. You may be doing something totally unrelated, when suddenly stage 4 – the 'eureka' moment happens.

Illumination – the moment when suddenly you are struck by the answer. Often it's so simple you wonder why you didn't think of it before.

You put on your logical head again and seek verification of your hunches and insights.

Motivate others to generate good ideas

Ideas are ephemeral – like butterflies, they flit through our minds, and if we do not have a net standing by to catch them then they fly away. Andrew Wood is an ideas catcher, who shows companies how to net employees' good ideas. He has spotted the potential revenue companies forego when they lose out on workers' innovative ways of thinking.

German employers are keen to recognize their employees' innovative ideas. About 600 of the largest companies, such as Mercedes, Porsche, Volkswagon and BMW, run schemes. Ideas are sent to headquarters and are scrutinized by a centralized team of managers who receive ongoing training on trends and evaluation methods. German staff prefer payment for their ideas, so recognition is heavily geared towards financial awards.

European companies give prizes of 15 to 25 per cent of first-year savings made from an implemented idea, whereas in North America and the UK, cash awards tend to be 10 per cent.

American employers favour non-monetary motivators – such as staff-recognition awards with lots of hand clapping and razzmatazz – which doesn't work with British staff.

British bosses opt for giving workers lunch, theatre tickets or tickets for sporting activities, plus financial awards.

In the Middle East, workers get only two weeks' holiday, and many prefer an award of several days' leave, so they can extend visits to relatives.

The award has to be something that workers want, otherwise they won't participate and employers lose out on potentially big ideas.

Incentive awards

Julian Richer's hi-fi chain Richer Sounds is the most prolific company in the UK for creative staff suggestions. Each employee averages 20 ideas a year, and 60 per cent are used. Small motivational awards, up to £25, can be made and suggestions implemented immediately. Ideas such as: 'We should install door bells at wheelchair height for disabled customers', may not save money, but contribute to customer service.

What motivates staff to submit ideas?

Siemens, the giant Munich-based electronics company, surveyed its staff to find out what motivated them to submit ideas. The results were:

* 'It's an opportunity to improve or help implement something.' (29 per cent)
* 'To ensure my own workplace security.' (24 per cent)
* 'To get an award.' (15 per cent)
* 'For someone to pay attention to my idea.' (13 per cent)
* 'To implement an idea without my supervisor's agreement.' (9 per cent)
* 'To receive recognition.' (4 per cent)
* 'To participate in special lotteries and raffles,' and 'additional awards for team suggestions.' (2 per cent)
* 'Responding to the encouragement of my supervisor.' (1 per cent)

[Courtesy of *London Evening Standard*, 'Just the Job', © Frances Coombes]

Ideas come from association and combination

Most of the ideas we get are not new, they come from associating different aspects of products, inventions and ideas produced by other people and putting them together in a way that is novel. Often the environment in which people work can be a hotbed for creative, inventive and imaginative ideas because people on the shopfloor can see exactly what the problems are.

* Shirley Langridge, a Post Office counters section worker, was concerned that queues were building up because short-sighted pensioners were forgetting their glasses. She came up with the simple but effective idea of introducing magnifying sheets in post offices attached to counters so that short-sighted people could see to fill in forms.

* Philip Barnes-Warden, a uniform services' support manager with the Metropolitan Police suggested recycling old police uniforms. The idea was taken onboard and now a recycling company provides a textile skip; clothes are sent to developing countries or recycled into padding for the motor industry. In addition to the annual savings of £12,000 on skip hire, the Met receives £65 per tonne from a recycling company for the clothing collected – which generates £6,500 a year.
* Detective Constable Steve Hobson, a community safety officer for Greater Manchester Police, came up with an idea for a safety video for people with learning difficulties, which has gone on sale throughout Australia, New Zealand and the South Pacific countries. He says: 'I get a real buzz out of coming up with ideas and seeing them actually come to fruition.' He has also come up with an idea for another video called Forceful Ideas which gives students advice on how to stay safe in the city. It tells them how to use products such as personal alarms that can be stretched across the back of a bedroom door and automatically sound if an intruder breaks the seal by opening the door.

Generating ideas to solve problems

Stimulate new ideas and fresh creative insights:
* Talk to people and see what they suggest. Often you will not be the only person with this problem.
* Describe the problem in another way.
* Decide what is the most important and real issue by constantly asking, 'Why is that so?'
* Listen to experts – what would they do?

Framing your ideas

To make sure that great ideas don't slip through the net, you need a framework that you can use to organize your ideas so that you can present them to interested parties. Start by brainstorming and asking yourself the following questions.

Solution generating technique

Write three sentences detailing:
 1 what the problem is
 2 how the problem has arisen
 3 what your desired outcome is.

Use these sentences as headings to flesh more detail under each. Then ask yourself questions such as:
   * Is a solution necessary?
   * What will happen if things stay the same?
   * What will solve the problem for me?
   * How will my suggestion resolve the problem?

Draw diagrams or pictures that will help others to understand your idea more clearly.

Estimate what the saving will be in time or money if the idea is implemented.

Generating good ideas – the creative process

The greatest minds in history have acknowledged the importance of imagination. Einstein said: 'Imagination is more important than knowledge.' Shakespeare wrote: 'Imagination makes man the paragon of animals.' Disraeli said: 'Imagination governs the world.'

Boost your creativity

On the opposite page is a creativity boosting exercise. Once you can achieve high scores for uses with single associations move on to combining two and then three unassociated objects, and finding all sorts of zany uses for them. Then when your brain is really buzzing, start working on a solution to your own particular challenge.

Following the exercise, there are a couple of simple but elegant examples of the type of solutions individuals can generate when using combining exercises to work on real problems.

Creativity boosting exercise

Spend 10 minutes a day increasing your ability to think creatively about the different ways in which everyday objects can be used. Aim to think of at least 30 ideas to do with each object, for example, a brick, a bin lid, a wheel, a paper bag, a dinner plate. Work under timed conditions and put some effort into it. Pick a different object each day and aim for a score of 30 or more. For example:

Day 1 – thirty things to do with a ladies' stocking

A ladies' stocking can be used: (1) to wear; (2) to tie up string beans; (3) to stuff cushions; (4) as a splint support; (5) as a water filter; (6) to catch tadpoles; (7) as a container for marbles; (8) as a cosh; (9) as a mask to rob a bank; (10) to keep hair in place.

Now you've got the picture – it's your turn. Pick an object and brainstorm as many different uses for it as possible.

Scoring Less than 10: unimaginative; 10–15: you're getting better; 15–19: good; 20–24: congratulations, you're really motoring; more than 25: you're a genius.

Creativity boosting example 1

British Telecom's Hereford Communications Centre was having problems because rabbits were continually tunnelling under perimeter fences and setting off intruder alarms.

Ingredients:
1 perimeter fence
2 rabbits
3 solution?

Pause here to think how you might solve the problem before moving to the solution.

Solution

Ian Collins, an employee at BT, came up with a simple but clever idea which solved the problem. He suggested burying ceramic pipes under fences to allow the rabbits to get in and out without compromising security. The idea worked.

Creativity boosting example 2

The vision of the Prison Service's security cameras was becoming obscured by insects and spiders, who found the camera housing ideal for nesting and spinning webs. Because surveillance cameras were located up high, it was time consuming for the staff to find ladders before wiping clean camera lenses.

Ingredients:
1. camera equipment
2. insects/spiders
3. solution?

Pause here to think how you might solve the problem before moving to the solution.

Solution

Prison Officer Les Kendall suggested applying a slippery coating to the housing. Spiders now find it impossible to keep a foothold and, to the relief of the Prison Service, are moving out.

An idea is only a notion – unless an action follows

Once you begin flexing your mental muscles and generating lots of ideas, follow up immediately with actions so you become used to achieving your goals on a regular basis. Start with small tasks first and work your way up to the biggies. Each small success will reinforce your belief in yourself as a winner.

If you have a brilliant idea about changing or finding a solution to a problem at work, how would you capture it and turn it into reality? Andrew Wood advises: 'To make sure that great ideas do not slip through the net, you need a framework to get your ideas

into a shape so that you can present them to interested parties.'
Start by brainstorming and asking yourself the questions in the
following section.

Capturing good ideas – the strategy

Write three sentences:
1 Detail what the problem is.
2 How has it arisen?
3 What is your desired outcome?

Use these sentences as headings to flesh out more detail under each. Then ask yourself questions such as:

* Is a solution necessary?
* What will happen if things stay the same?
* What will solve the problem for me?
* How will my suggestion resolve the problem?

Draw diagrams or pictures that will help others to understand your idea more clearly. Estimate what the saving will be in time or money if the idea is implemented.

Walt Disney's creativity strategy

Walt Disney, whose animated films charmed generations of children, would separate out the roles of 'dreamer', 'realist' and 'critic' when generating creative ideas, so that each aspect could be focused on and explored separately. At the 'dreamer' stage he would brainstorm ideas without inhibition; he would then switch to the 'realist', a more practical role, to work out the framework and details of how things would be done. Finally, he would become the 'critic' as he checked and looked for inconsistencies in his work.

You can use the Disney strategy:

* alone or when you want to generate creativity within a team
* when you have an idea and are in conflict between the practicalities of implementing it and the dream
* when you want to test several ideas to see how they might be realized.

If you are working in a group you could ask people to take on the different roles and view ideas from 'dreamer', 'realist' and 'critic' viewpoints. Ask the dreamer to tell you about the possibilities of an idea. Then ask the realist to imagine what would be involved in turning the idea into reality. Finally, ask the critic to evaluate the strengths and weaknesses of the idea.

Generate ideas and turn them into reality

Create a sense of urgency about whatever you want to achieve. Some people tend to procrastinate at the ideas stage; give them a month to come up with an idea and it will take a month, give them a day and they will hatch it in a day. Generate the necessary pressure by giving yourself challenging but reasonable deadlines for objectives and stick to them.

Choose projects that fire you with enthusiasm, rather than those that drain your energy. Enthusiasm plays a major part in helping people to generate creative ideas. If you are fired up you will be able to imagine, structure, build and turn your ideas into reality more quickly. So make sure you have an ample supply of the excitement factor. People rarely succeed at things that do not excite them.

5

sharpen your thinking

Wherever you are now in life you have reached that place as a result of the thinking and planning you have done to date. So are you where you want to be? Only when you know what you seek to change in your life can you start making effective changes. It may be that you need an entirely different career, or a real challenge. If you do not know what you are looking for then you cannot plan your route map to success.

Consider this: if there was a miracle tonight and you woke up in the morning and everything was just the way you wanted it to be – how would you know it had happened?

What are the things you would see, hear, feel and believe that would tell you a miracle had happened?

What would achieving your goals give you that you do not already have right now?

Write down the missing information; it is your criteria for success.

> *'Planning without action is futile.
> Action without planning is fatal.'*
>
> (Business maxim)

Learning new skills

Top performers realize that there is a limit to the relationship between working harder and longer to increase effectiveness. Initially working hard and long may be exhilarating, but over time there is a price to pay in terms of stress, exhaustion and burnout. Constantly relying on adrenalin to get you through a project is destructive and can be seen as self-induced substance abuse.

By working smarter, rather than harder, we can harness more of our thinking ability in order to achieve our aims and look after our future well-being. Standing still in self-development terms is no longer an option, we will always need skills to advance us in our careers.

We never fully develop all our talents

No matter what age we are, we all have talents that are not fully developed. Successful people realize that they are the only people who can improve their results, so they plan ahead. They start with a goal in the future to aim for and then devise a plan of action by systematically thinking backwards to the present time and working out what resources, skills, abilities, tools and techniques they will require to achieve their aim.

Script your life

Think ahead five years to a time when you have successfully reached a main goal and write the script of what has happened in the interim. Work backwards to the present day, writing down the steps you took to get to where you are now.

* How did you get to your result?
* What skills and talents did you use?

> * Are you using all those skills now to your maximum potential?
> * List the reasons for the success you have had.
>
> This will give you more ideas on what you need to do to achieve greater success.

Get leverage when setting future goals

When you change a car wheel the leverage exerted by the jack is what allows you to lift an object 40 times your own weight. In business and sales, leverage, also known as the 80/20 rule, can come from identifying and concentrating on a critical few customers, rather than applying equal energy and attention to all.

To leverage your time when completing a task, remember that 80 per cent of the returns from your daily 'to do' list will come from 20 per cent of the items you have listed and often from just one item. Avoid falling into the 'busy trap' of racing around completing lots of small tasks that may be easy or insistent or satisfying but ultimately achieve little. Instead focus on the most important task, even though it may not be urgent. Ask yourself: 'Which of these tasks relates directly to my goals?', 'Which will still matter five years from now?'

> If there was a miracle tonight and you woke up in the morning and everything was just the way you wanted it to be ... how would you know it had happened?
> * What would you see, hear, feel and believe that would tell you a miracle had happened?
> * What would achieving your goal give you that you do not already have?

We all have individual patterns of behaviour that are instantly recognizable to ourselves and to others. Over time our repetitive actions accumulate and we get results. The actions that you have taken over time, have built into the results that you have now.

5 sharpen your thinking

What are your criteria for success?

What are your criteria for achieving a better job or a better life? Identify the feeling you want to have when things are working well rather than focusing on the problem.

How will you know you have achieved what you want?

Your evidence might be, 'I will feel more positive in meetings with my bosses, and I will see myself looking and acting confidently, and hear myself contributing to discussions.'

Strategic planning

The hardest part of developing and employing a strategic plan is having the confidence to use it and the ability to stick to it once you have your plan in place. This is where the real work of building up a combination of the skills of evaluation and taking actions begins. The most common questions that start to arise at this point are:

* How do you stay on track?
* How do you know that you are looking for the right thing?
* How do you know when you have slipped away from thinking strategically?

Only by constantly questioning your ongoing decisions and monitoring your results, both good and bad, can you begin to know what works and what doesn't. Question everything you do.

* Were your decisions good?
* How accurate were your evaluations of situations?
* Were the tactics you used sound?
* What worked and what didn't? Make a list and keep it to hand for your next plan.
* What would you do differently next time?
* Was your outcome successful?

If your outcome was not wholly successful, was this due to:

Lack of skill	Lack of knowledge
Could you acquire this ingredient? Over- or under-estimation of your abilities?	Did you fail to get important pieces of information?
Lack of resources	**Lack of forethought**
Was an important ingredient that is missing necessary to assure a good outcome?	Has something happened that you were not prepared for and had no plan for dealing with?

It is vital for us to be aware of our pattern of strategic and tactical thinking if we are to be able to improve on it. We need strategy to keep our tactics on course, and we need techniques to help us evaluate the deeper consequence of our tactical decisions.

Increase your pattern recognition skills

It is not just our own thinking and decision-making patterns that we need to record, there are patterns going on all around us. Early in life we begin to recognize similar trends, patterns of behaviour, and mental pictures of recurring past events.

Traders who buy and sell stocks and shares notice trends in buying and selling patterns; mortgage lenders can predict customer behaviour patterns; we can predict our family's or workmate's behaviour based on what we know of their recurring habits. If we are about to try a new venture we can predict the outcome based on what has gone before and past results in similar situations. All this saves us from having to re-invent the wheel.

If we can recognize a pattern we can:
* evaluate it
* test it to see if it works
* isolate the parts of it that don't work and change them for some better tactics.

If we develop the ability to recognize meaningful patterns, it means when we tackle a problem we never have to start from scratch. Instead we instinctively look for past parallels. We see if we can work out a recipe similar to someone else's from those slightly different ingredients we are working with.

Develop the habit of using outcome thinking every time you are planning ahead. Anything from a simple to-do list to strategic organizational planning should have planned objectives set.

Set clear goals and outcomes

Setting objectives helps you think through complex and changing situations. Having clear goals and outcomes helps you achieve the results you want. Set goals and keep written outlines which give you a plan of the actions you need to take to achieve your outcomes.

Ensure your goals are SMART. Start with an aim or a goal in mind. An aim is an objective, a marker, an outcome on the way to a final achievement. Every outcome is made up of sub-outcomes which build up to a final achievement. An end is a final outcome or goal.

Your goals should be:

Specific   A short, specific, simple description of the outcome you want.
Measurable   Goals should be measurable, meaningful to you. There should be more than one way to achieve them.
Achievable   Describe goals in the present tense, as if they are happening now and are achievable.
Realistic   Your goals should be responsible, realistic and right for you.
Timeframe   State a timeframe in which you will achieve your goals.

To be excellent in everything you do, your goal must be to become conscious of your thinking processes and the actions you take that spring from them. Notice how successful your results are and then constantly seek to improve them.

Develop flexible thinking skills

To become a flexible thinker capable of focusing on the 'big picture' or whole plan in one instant and 'small detail specific' information in another, it is important that we can 'chunk' our thinking up and down at will. Big picture thinking will let us see what the whole project will look like when it is finished. Setting your objectives requires that you change your thinking and begin to think in detail about how each of your objectives will be met.

Chunk your thinking

'Chunking' is a process of grouping information into large or small amounts, 'chunks', depending on the type of information we want to obtain. You may hear people described as 'big picture thinkers', which means they are easily able to visualize and have an overview of a whole situation.

The most able thinkers are skilled in changing their thinking patterns at will in order to ask questions that shed light on a task, situation, event, project or outcome in lots of different ways. This type of thinking lets you gain more insight into situations from seeing a subject from lots of different points of view.

Chunking down information

In computer language a chunk is a description of a piece of information of a particular size. Chunking means to break down information into smaller parts.

To chunk up when thinking, means to go from small detail-specific questions such as, 'How specifically will I ...?' to big picture thinking which involves how the whole process or project works, for example, 'This wind tunnel is built for the purpose of ....'

To chunk down is to go from seeing the finished project, the big picture, to homing in on individual aspects, small component parts that form part of the whole. Chunking down large objectives into smaller goals makes them easier to deal with.

Having the flexibility to chunk your questions up or down in any situation is one of the most valuable skills you can acquire. Chunking helps you organize your thinking so you can handle more information in different ways.

> You already chunk information when you remember phone numbers. You group the regional part of the number together and then split the rest of the numbers into chunks to make them more memorable.

Chunking up and down at will gives you the flexibility to become adept at categorizing information. You can classify things into groups, and move your thinking from the specific (small chunk) to the general (big picture) to obtain lots of new information which would not be available to you if you stuck to your regular thinking pattern.

Situations where using chunking is helpful

* Setting goals.
* Negotiating.
* Team building.
* Resolving conflict.
* Intervention or problem solving.
* Preparing a presentation and ensuring it is given to the audience in the right 'bite-sized chunks' for them to understand and assimilate.

How to chunk up your thinking

To chunk up for solutions to big picture outcomes, ask questions which require people to examine their beliefs, values and what is important to them. Ask:

* What is important to you about …?
* What would motivate you in order to …?
* What does having this outcome achieve for you?
* What is an example of …?
* What have you learned?
* For what purpose?

How to chunk down your thinking

To chunk down to find out about specific outcome explanations, ask questions which elicit small detail explanations:

> * What stops you ...?
> * What is an example of this?
> * Who/what/when/where/how ... specifically?

Think of chunking up and down

When you have a problem that seems daunting think of chunking it down into smaller more manageable sections. This enables you to focus on one specific area at a time and find solutions, before moving on to the next task.

If you feel overwhelmed by too much detail then chunk up to find the purpose or meaning for what you are doing. Getting the big picture will give you an overview so you can define what you are doing and why you need to do it.

Chunking up and down skills are vital for analysing problems, finding the best approach to new situations and setting new and more challenging goals.

6
the power of setting goals

You are more likely to reach your goals when they become steps in an overall strategy.

Know what you want and in what context you want to excel in. Have a route map for getting there. Set recognizable markers along the way that will let you know that you are on target. Establish that what you are doing is not in conflict with other goals you set.

Stack your goals in the same direction, so that they flow together towards your ultimate aims. Visualize reaching your goals and run lots of action replays, so that you taste and see what your achievements will look like when you hold them in the palm of your hand.

Begin with a goal you burn to achieve, something difficult enough to excite you, but not beyond your abilities.

'Saddle your dreams afore you ride 'em'

Mary Webb (1881–1927)

Being successful at reaching your goals is the biggest and most exciting gift you can give yourself. To achieve fulfilling goals, you first have to know what you want from life and have the inner awareness of how these things connect to your values and beliefs, and ultimately your life's purpose. Without goal setting there can be no success, so commit your desires to the forefront of your mind to make your purpose a reality.

The power of setting goals

While purpose is a long-range target and usually far ahead, goals are shorter. You may have a goal to set up your own business, to run a marathon, get married or increase your learning. Any of these aims might take several years to achieve, but they are all markers along the road to your purpose. You do not stop everything when you get there because these aims are not your ultimate destination.

How often do you set goals?

If you feel bored, uninspired, or that life lacks sparkle then check to see when you last set yourself some interesting goals. It could be that you do not set goals and have got into the habit of going along with the ebb and flow of life's events.

If you do not set your own goals, that doesn't mean you do not achieve targets. You may be part of someone else's dreams and purpose, a cog in your employer's production line or your partner's or family's aspirations.

When you know how to maintain your level of motivation, how you set your goals, and how to follow through with positive actions, you hold the key to success in every area of your life. The art of consciously goal setting is one of the most invaluable mental tools you will ever possess.

Means, motive and opportunity

To set goals and achieve them, you need to employ some of the techniques used by detectives. First you need to know whether you have the means, motive and opportunity to reach your goal.

* **Means:** Do you have the requirements such as skill, time, money, connections and knowledge that will help you reach your aim?
* **Motive:** Do you want your outcome enough to pay the price? Are you prepared not to waiver or be distracted from your goal and to follow through until completion?
* **Opportunity:** Do you have the opportunity to go for it, and how much control do you have over the outcome? Although you are unlikely to have complete control over a business or relationship outcome, the more control you have in your power to influence the outcome, the more likely you are to achieve your aim.

Once you have established that all systems are based on the means, motive and opportunity ingredients, it is your beliefs about yourself and your power and determination to make things happen that will determine how successful you are.

Successful goal-achieving strategies are not just useful for business purposes. They link in to every other area of your life, be it financial, career, social, family, mental, physical or spiritual. How we picture ourselves, whether it's as a success or failure, ultimately affects our level of confidence and self-esteem and our beliefs about the things we are capable of achieving in the future.

Success for many people comes through the career they choose or the talents that they offer in exchange for money and/or recognition.

If we really do choose the lives we want to live then here's an interesting question. Are you, right now, sitting in the location you want to be, doing the work you want to do because it interests or excites you? Are you exchanging your skills for money and recognition – or are you just doing a job for money?

What are goals?

* Goals are specific, they are actions you can take that lead in the direction of your purpose.
* Your goals should be personal to you, although they may link into someone else's goals.
* Goals should be interesting and inspire you.
* Goals are measurable, which allows you to judge how much progress you have made towards reaching your target.
* Goals should be achievable, not so easy that they don't tax you, not so hard that you regularly fail to reach them and so become disillusioned.
* Your goals should be realistic and fit in with who you are and what you are capable of. If you are a chronic asthmatic then it might be wise to pick a goal other than wanting to run the London Marathon, although there might be benefits to improving your fitness in less rigorous ways.
* Goals should be set within a definite timeframe. They should also have definite markers along the route so you can tell if you are doing well or if you may need to change some of your tactics.

Organizations and businesses often fit lots of goals within other goals that align to a purpose.

Align your goals so they flow in the same direction

* Know what you want and in what context you want to excel in.
* Have a plan or route map for getting there.
* Have recognizable markers along the way that will let you know whether you are on target.
* Know that what you are doing is not in conflict with other goals you have. (It's amazing how easily this can happen. For instance, do you know people who are food conscious and take supplements to improve their health yet still

smoke 20 cigarettes a day?) Work out a way to stack your goals in the same direction so that they all flow together in the direction of your ultimate purpose.
* Visualize your goal and run lots of action replays so that you will recognize what your achievement will look like when you reach it.

Our goals are not set in isolation, they are usually connected to and involve other people, things, and situations. Constantly ask yourself, 'When I achieve this outcome, what else might it lead to, where else might it take me?'

Choose a promising goal
1 Think of ten things you'd really like to do.
2 Imagine yourself doing each one in turn.
3 Now narrow your choices down to the three most possible.
4 Don't you just want to get started on one of them right now?

Set your outcomes

Think about something you really burn to achieve, something that is difficult enough to excite you, but not totally beyond your abilities. From your list of goals is there one that it is imperative for you to reach now, one that hinges to lots of other important aims in your life?

Clearly defining your goals is the first step
1 **What do you want?** You may already have some definite goals in mind but, if you don't, then now is the time to get them. From your column headings of Business, Work, Money, Health or Relationships, pick something that is important to you in relation to your life's ambitions.
2 **Imagine you already have your outcome.** What are the things that you will see, hear, feel and experience that will let you know you have achieved your goal? Athletes practise these sort of actions every day, imagining they have hit the ball, run the race, lifted the weight, lived the experience

many times before the actual event. In this way they use all of their sensory apparatus to see things they might not otherwise see, play through and correct different actions in their imagination, and feel all the feelings associated with performing brilliantly and achieving success. When they walk on to a pitch, into a stadium, up to a pool table or into a boxing ring, they have success hard-wired into their neurology. When it's time to perform, even in teams, they don't have to think 'Who shall I pass the ball to?' and 'Will he be there?', each person's actions are synchronized to achieving the same outcome.

Check for any side effects you haven't thought of

1 **Context: In what circumstances do you want this outcome?** Business, work, home, social? Are there any circumstances that you wouldn't want it? For instance, your aim might be to acquire better leadership skills so you can take on a more challenging role in your work. But would you want to carry those skills over to dealings with your friends or family? Be aware that your change in thinking style and behaviour in work, if carried into other areas of your life, might change the dynamics of your relationships.

2 **Impact: How will having this outcome affect the people around you?** Business associates, work colleagues, partner, family, friends? Sometimes relationships break up because one partner is striving to be more successful while the other stays the same. If your goal will affect your whole family then involve them and get them to buy into what you are doing at an early stage.

3 **Cost analysis: What will you gain from having this outcome?** What do you get from what you are presently doing? Will you lose anything you value by achieving your outcome? Some business entrepreneurs pay the price of losing their first marriage when they undertake a goal

because their beliefs and values evolve while their partner's remain the same.

Have you the control, resources and time you need?

Now do you still want this outcome?

Frame your goal plan

Your goals should fit into an overall strategy. Write them down so that you can refer to them and modify your methods according to any changes in circumstances.

Goals that are set in relation to others are more likely to be completed, even when the going gets tough, whereas ones set in isolation are more likely to be abandoned if things don't go to plan.

Keep things simple to start with and do not over-plan. It is possible to become overwhelmed with the details of how to achieve your goals and to end up feeling disconnected from your final outcome.

Initially practise simple goals, over short timescales. Break them down until you reach an action you can take immediately, which will give you lots of small successes from the outset. If you imagine having achieved your goal and then think backwards in time you can work out the progressional steps you took to get there. From this action you can work out whether you have the resources necessary to start your plan moving and also to know what is the next step to take you towards your goal.

Tips for goal setting

Break down your goals into small chunks

A complete project, such as breaking into and saturating a sales market, or being slim, supple and active, or earning a million pounds may seem daunting. So break down your steps into chunks and be determined each day to take some small steps towards achieving your goal.

Focus on the progress you are making each day

To write this book and fit it into an already full-time schedule, I kept a time-log diary with a page for each day that I worked on the project. From noticing what worked and what didn't, I decided that I would fit at least five 20-minute segments of time to inputting on the computer in the early morning when I was at my most productive. I also logged each day how easy or difficult I found the progress. Whenever I reached sticking points I was able to look back and remember what I was thinking, doing and feeling when I had been working well and found the going enjoyable.

Think about your goal constantly

See yourself achieving your goal and run action movies in your mind. Use all your senses of seeing, hearing, feeling, taste and smell to associate with your picture more fully. See your movie from different angles, so that if there are obstacles you can view the problem from another perspective.

Commit your goals to writing

Keep your goals simple and use concrete words. 'I want to be thinner' is not a goal, it is a wish. 'I want to be 2 kg thinner in three weeks' gives you a timeframe and target. Write down the specific markers you will see, hear and feel, such as 'I will feel fitter and look fabulous in a new outfit', that will let you know that you have reached your aim.

Work smarter – not harder

Often it's necessary to work extremely hard to get a project started. But if this means you are constantly working under pressure, working long hours and lacking sleep, your standard of work and ability to think strategically will suffer. Don't get so tied up in your project that you don't have time for anything else. You know where you're headed, so be good to yourself along the way. Take some time to smell the roses, and give yourself some enjoyment and lots of little rewards.

Do a look back exercise
At the end of every project do a look back exercise, and review and write down what worked well and what didn't work. Look at ways of getting better and smoother at what you do, and of improving your efficiency.

7
take control of how you think

Sometimes, when stressed, we automatically reconnect to past feelings of dread experienced in childhood. It may be 30 years later and the person is a successful executive, but when faced with a deadline, or challenge, the old feelings of panic re-emerge, just as when handing in a classroom essay and expecting bad comments.

Athletes and business people, with the help of professional sports and personal development coaches, are used to capitalizing on accessing their feel-good state. They anchor their memories of success and have a powerful tool to use in stressful situations to reconnect with their confident and winning thinking patterns.

You can take control of how you think in an amazing way that will enable you to achieve high class performances in your own field.

Would it be useful if you could anchor a confident state in a difficult situation on command? With practice, you can have that skill.

For maximum impact notice listeners' thinking styles

Thinking style tips

If you are selling your product or idea to someone, the better you understand how people think and comprehend their internal drivers, the more able you are to influence and predict their behaviour.

* There are people who move 'away from pain' and at the other end of the scale there are those who are motivated to move 'towards pleasure'.
* Some customers want a new product to be 'different' and others look for 'sameness' to whatever they are using now.
* There are also 'sameness with exception' people who like to know the product is similar to the one they had before and then to hear words such as 'improvement', 'better', 'more', 'less'.

Questions to elicit what motivates a person

You can find out what motivates a person by asking them a question such as:

* Why did you decide to change your last job?
* Why did you change your last partner?

Choose a question where they tell you why they changed something.

People who move towards pleasure will tell you, 'Well, I saw this great job, it offered a lot of potential for me to do the sort of things I wanted', and they will offer a list of criteria.

People who move away from pain will say, 'Well, I couldn't stand my job anymore, and so I left.'

When it comes to partners the story is similar. People who move away from pain will say, 'Well, I couldn't stand it anymore so I got out.'

The person who is motivated towards a goal might say, 'Well, I found a better partner, so I grabbed the chance to be happy.'

Don't assume that people who run 'away from' strategies will do any less well than those who run 'towards' fulfilment; both types can be phenomenally successful but are motivated towards their goals in different ways.

We run similar thinking patterns in similar situations

Some people naturally move towards goals – others move away from pain. These are recognizable thinking styles that people run in similar contexts. These methods of organizing information are patterns of thinking and behaviour that are outside our awareness, yet they have a major effect on how we respond to situations in the world.

Knowing how habitual thinking patterns work will give you a better understanding of how you are motivated. This is useful information for:

* when you are setting your goals
* knowing other people's thinking styles
* building rapport with others.

Recognize people's different thinking styles

Recognizing your own and other people's thinking styles can help you understand better how you are motivated; it can help predict your future behaviour in recognizable circumstances.

Understanding thinking styles allows you to plan ahead how you might interact with other people, and alter your behaviour to get the best results from others and the outcomes you desire. The list below shows the characteristic behaviour of people who fall within each thinking style.

Checklist of thinking styles

Move away from pain
- Focus on problems.
- Talk about what they do not want to happen.
- Are motivated by negative consequences.
- Often have difficulty defining their goals.

Move towards pleasure
- Respond to incentives.
- Are motivated by achievements.
- May find it difficult to recognize negative consequences.

Motivated by necessity
- Often display driven behaviour.
- Strong ideas on how things should be done.
- Motivated by clearcut, recognizable methods.

Motivated by options and possibility
- Want choices, lots of options.
- Good at thinking up new ways of doing things.
- Motivated by new challenges.

Internally focused
- Respond to the content of the communication.
- Do not notice or respond to others' emotional behaviour.
- Do not easily build rapport with others.

Attention focused on others
- Respond to the people around them.
- Good rapport builders.
- Take responsibility for the way that other people feel.

Sort for similarities
- Will notice what is the same in a situation.
- Will often repeat a story similar to the one you tell.
- Use words like, 'just like me', 'the same', 'similar'.

Sort for what is different
* Notice what is different.
* Sort for what is missing.
* Can be fault finders.

Big chunk thinker
* Takes a global view of an idea or situation.
* Does not pay attention to the small details.
* Can overlook things that do not fit into an overall plan.

Small chunk thinker
* Good at remembering and handling details.
* May lack an overall framework to relate an idea to.
* Want to be familiar with the process of doing things.

Identify your thinking patterns

Look at the checklist of thinking styles descriptions above and mentally replay some recent situations in your head and how you reacted at the time. Ask yourself which type of thinking you habitually use – that is your thinking style.

Check where you are on the continuum using the thinking styles patterns below. Draw an X on the line at the point where you think you function in that particular thinking style.

Away from pain	←——————→	Towards pleasure
Necessity	←——————→	Possibility
Self-referenced	←——————→	Respond to others
Sort for similarities	←——————→	Look for difference
Big picture thinker	←——————→	Small chunk thinker

Thinking styles are useful predictors of behaviour, and recognizing and understanding them allows you to make crucial distinctions about how to interact with people. They are guides to behaviour only – no one is exclusively programmed to behave in a certain way. And we can all, with practice, learn to change unhelpful or irritating behaviour.

What are you saying to yourself?

Away from pain vs. Towards pleasure

Did I see this problem coming but put it off until it could no longer be avoided? Or did I see the possibilities in the situation and move towards making changes?

Necessity vs. Possibility

Is this a problem because **I think it is**, or because **someone else has told me it is**?

Self-referenced vs. Respond to others

Am I worried about the consequences **for myself**, other people or both?

Sort for similarities vs. Look for difference

Is this problem **similar to** or **different from** other problems I've faced before? If so, how is it similar/different?

Big picture thinker vs. small chunk thinker

If you are thinking 'this always happens to me', you are generalizing. Asking yourself why this specific thing is happening is a more useful question that will generate more answers.

Now think about what happened to make you change your mind and decide that you could reach your goal. What changed in the sights and sounds and feelings you were experiencing to help you achieve your outcome? Highlight those sensations in another colour and transfer to your blueprint.

Once you understand your own behaviour patterns when faced with problems and how you solved them in the past, you can record this information and let it work for you to propel you more quickly towards your goals.

To change a habit look at what holds it in place

Limiting styles of thinking and behaviour make life more difficult because they can lead to stuck situations. If we can notice and categorize the sort of habitual thinking that may be stopping us from reaching goals, we can replace it with something new that will keep all the benefits of the old habit and still get us the outcome we want.

8

model success strategies

When you can identify people's thinking and behaviour patterns in advance, you can determine or influence how they make their future choices.

To attract more customers to your restaurant, ask some people to talk you through their thinking process for choosing a restaurant meal. Notice sensory language they used: Did they get a **'feeling'** first that told them they were hungry? Did they **'see'** the food in their mind's eye? Did they **'talk'** to themselves and imagine **'tasting'** each dish in turn? Build up a sensory sequence of how each person makes their choice.

How might this information be useful? To attract **'visual'** diners, show bright pictures of food. **'Auditory'** diners want written menus with sensuous and appetizing descriptions of meals. **'Touchy feelies'** are attracted to lighting and décor that creates a warm and inviting atmosphere.

To triple your customers, ensure your restaurant meets the criteria for all sensory types.

Noticing successful strategies

If you can work out how another person can do something that you yearn to do, it opens up a world full of possibilities for you. Knowing that you can observe, map and reproduce the strategies people use to become masters in their fields gives you a blueprint for success. You can model the skills of the most talented people around you and use these skills to achieve your personal goals and desires in life.

You might want to be thin, get promotion, be a better shopper, lover, businessperson, sportsperson, entrepreneur or host; you might want to do almost anything! Chapter 7 looked at habits and behaviour patterns that people display and why people do things; here we look at how they do them.

All professional athletes have coaches who teach them to notice and build on other successful sportspeople's strategies. Many of these strategies are also adapted and used in business to enhance people's teamwork, sales performance, negotiating, or communications skills. Every franchise outlet that opens on a high street is modelled on the successful practices of businesses elsewhere.

How do you do that?

> If you're in sales, human resources, training, or any business which requires advanced communication skills you can capitalize on the magic of understanding why people do the things they do. Get the action habit — you don't need to wait until conditions for learning new skills are perfect. Whenever you see somebody with a really good skill, one that you'd like to acquire, get into the habit of asking, 'How do you do that?'

Knowing what motivates other people to make their choices can help you change your life to be just the way you want it. Suppose you want to be slim, trim and active: you could model a range of slim people's thinking and behaviour and find out what it is about their strategies that keeps them slim. Ask them how they decide when it is time to eat.

Similarly, if you want to be a successful entrepreneur, spend an evening at an entrepreneurs' gathering and build up a picture of what makes them different from the rest of the herd. Entrepreneurs tend to be proactive, they make decisions quickly and are also prepared to take the sort of risks other people might not. They tend to think big and aim high.

How do you score as a high achiever?

To find out how you score as a high achiever, for each of the statements below rate yourself on a scale of 1–10.

High achievers have a passion for what they are doing.	
Their goals are supported by their emotions.	
They believe their actions can make a difference.	
Life is about seizing chances and learning from experiences.	
The successful person's goal is overcoming challenges.	
They have the ability to observe, identify and adapt other people's strategies for their own uses.	
Their energy and enthusiasm comes from being on purpose and working towards their goals.	
Successful people are master communicators.	

If you commit to improving your skill, talents and abilities, you can increase your score for any of the above.

Your beliefs about what you are capable of doing give you leverage

> * Write down ten positive beliefs that you hold about yourself which have supported you (i.e. I'm a good ..., I will be successful because ..., I can do this because ....)
> * Now write down ten negative beliefs that you have held which have limited you (i.e. I'm not smart enough ..., I'm not good enough ..., I can't do it ....) Think about devising a simple modelling project which will provide you with the next step towards 'doing it', and repeatedly ask yourself 'What would happen if I could do it?'
>
> Keep your list and throughout this chapter think about what type of skills you might want to acquire that would help you move any items in the negative column to the positive. Systematically seek to improve your skills and performance capabilities and confidence in those areas.

Modelling success at work – blueprinting technique

Ann Fuller-Good, of training consultancy FOCUS Group, runs workshops where management and staff discover what makes people excel at work. She says, 'If you want to be successful, find a successful person and find out how they did it. If one person is good at a task because they have an interesting idea, that may not necessarily be a great way to do things. But if ten people have done the task in the same way, and they are all successful, you are getting close to excellence.'

> Eurostar has used this success blueprinting technique to train control staff who managed the rail terminal at Waterloo in London. Fuller-Good says, 'The aim was to find out what made excellent terminal controllers, and then give their colleagues the opportunity to try out the same thinking styles.'

Blueprinting excellence is more than taking on someone else's habits. You need to understand the beliefs that person holds that makes them outstanding. At workshops in other companies Fuller-Good studied people who make excellent leaders and discovered that the overriding belief they held was: 'There is more than one way of doing things.' She says, 'They believed that if they didn't get the result they wanted they could try a different approach. This belief manifested in the way they paid attention to achieving results.'

Fuller-Good says, 'If you're an admin person who would like to become a manager, then find someone who has the skills you'd like to be good at, say multitasking, or organizing things in chaotic situations. The questions to ask that person to bring out their underlying beliefs are: "How do you do this thing you're good at? And when you do it, what is important to you?"'

Before adopting someone else's belief, it is important you choose it consciously, and practise holding it for a while. Ask yourself, 'How will holding this belief benefit me? Can I accept and feel comfortable with it?' If you can, then one of the best ways to make a belief your own is repetition. Stick the message somewhere prominent and repeat it ten times a day. It usually takes three weeks of repetition for a new belief to become embedded. Notice how quickly the belief begins to alter the way you think when dealing with work situations.

Are some people born with a success gene? Fuller-Good says, 'No, but some people have early life experiences that seem to motivate them to achieve more than others. These are people who believe they will be successful and work towards that vision. They don't fear failure, they see it as a challenge, and believe they will overcome all obstacles.'

Is success worth the effort? You bet it is! Why not aim for it and see?

[Courtesy of Associated Newspapers, *London Evening Standard*, 'Just the Job', © Frances Coombes]

Start with simple observable skills that are easy to acquire

What sort of skills could you use that would motivate you and enhance your beliefs about your abilities or advance your career and take you to the top? You don't have to re-invent the wheel and come up with totally original ideas. Start mining the attributes you see in the people around you, initially learning skills which are relatively easy to acquire.

Some typical observable skills you might find at work

There are bound to be people in your workplace who have talents for particular aspects of their job. Modelling skills requires that instead of thinking 'I wonder why they're good at that?' or 'I wish I could do it like that', you move to a point of active curiosity and find out exactly *how* they do it.

Everyday examples of where you can start to model skills

There will be people all around you who are displaying the skills you would like. Regard your colleagues and isolate particular skills you might like to have. Some simple, easy and worthwhile skills to acquire from the people around you might be:

* how to make good decisions
* techniques for solving problems
* drawing spider diagrams to aid your creativity
* taking control of a situation
* how to ask for help
* how to say 'no'
* handling interruptions
* tips for saving time
* chairing successful meetings
* structuring reports
* speed reading techniques

* organizing your email system
* asking precision questions
* listening for what is really important
* dealing with a cluttered desk
* how to organize yourself
* planning situations in advance
* dealing with the unexpected.

Modelling

When you start to model a new skill or behaviour, you should keep a note of the things you will see, hear and feel when you achieve your success. Chart your progress by consulting and updating your attributes list regularly to see which of your beliefs have moved columns.

Notice small skills that are easy to acquire

Choose ten small practice skills that you really want to acquire from your colleagues. Acquiring these skills will make a visible difference to your overall performance at work. The question to ask to elicit people's strategy for doing the things they do well is 'How do you do that?'

If a strategy can be described, it can be taught and learned

The more we know about how a person who demonstrates the kind of excellence we want to have, the easier it becomes to follow their way of working and incorporate their strategies into our working life. Simple physical, observable skills are easiest to start with to learn and practise the process. Modelling shows us that it is not simply an accident, or good luck, that some people can do some things exceptionally well, while others may find it difficult. Modelling an excellent practitioner is a wonderful way to learn.

Easy skills to acquire

Do it now fever. You may have a colleague who, when given a task, takes-off like a whippet at the starting gate to complete it. If you are not as highly motivated, but would like to be, it may be worth noticing what is happening when this person is given a command. If you are a person who thinks, 'Do I really need to do this task, is it absolutely necessary?', 'I will sit on it for a day or two to think it through,' then get curious enough to ask them 'What happens in your brain, what do you think when you are given a new task?', 'How do you do what you do?' Find out what is going on mentally and physically for them when they are given a new task to perform. Notice particularly, and write down, the beliefs they hold about doing tasks straight away.

Acquire small incremental skills

Acquiring small incremental skills, like the everyday ones that are being performed well all around you, can change your performance from average to outstanding. If you become proficient at a dozen new strategies along with 'do it now fever', you are much more likely to be noticed and to accelerate your career path.

When you understand what causes successful behaviour and can repeat these patterns of thinking and behaviour at will, you will become consistently better at gathering effective strategies and making them your own.

Experience has structure

> If someone else can do something that you want to, then find that successful person and model him or her and how they do it. Modelling becomes exciting once you realize that a skill that might have taken months to learn can be acquired in a very short time.

Modelling other people's success skills and winning strategies will expand your potential to bring about similar successes. It will give you a deeper understanding of how people achieve excellence than textbook learning ever could. You also acquire new insight into the behaviour, beliefs, state of mind and sensory awareness that make up the whole experience when a person is engaged in the process that leads to their successful outcomes.

Think of modelling when you:
* want to be able to repeat a past performance when you have done something well and do not know how you've done it (self-modelling)
* want to learn a new skill or improve an existing one
* meet someone who is exceptionally good at a particular skill or talent and you want to find out more about how they do it
* want to emulate other people's successes
* want to change parts of what you have done, which might not have been successful, and keep the other parts that worked well.

Your models are all around you

> Is there someone with a really useful skill that you would like to model? One person might be a good organizer, another good at making quick decisions. You don't have to find someone who's a genius and excels at everything, only someone who excels in the activity you choose to model.

Begin to notice what it is that other people are doing when they are performing at their best.

9

pick a skill you want to acquire

Most people are only five or six skills away from achieving the successes they want in life. Which skills will you model to increase your range of possibilities? Start with easy to acquire everyday abilities that people around you display. Pick a skill you might notice and want to acquire:

How to pay or receive compliments.

Making good decisions quickly.

Capturing the essence of a book or a complex situation in a nutshell.

The ability to assemble flat-pack furniture.

Sorting clutter.

Stopping mind-chatter and becoming focused.

Leadership skills.

When modelling someone's skill, ask them 'How do you do that skill so brilliantly?' Listen, and observe what they do and the order they do it in. What are they thinking, believing and saying to themselves as they perform the task?

What are the skills that would change your life, and who can you model who's got them?

Success strategies that work

Whole industries such as sports performance enhancement, therapies, education, business management, sales, coaching, team development and just about any area of endeavour where people seek tools and techniques to enhance human performance, use techniques to model human excellence. Yet there is little written for the general reader who might want to self-improve in a few chosen areas using modelling techniques.

Choose a skill

Once you focus on a skill you want to acquire you get new insights into the behaviour, beliefs, state of mind and sensory experiences that make up the whole experience when a person is performing a task at their best. There are thousands of skills permutations you can model. It is important that the skill you choose to model is one that you really want to learn, rather than something on which to practise. Being curious about the process you want to learn about will make it more interesting and memorable to you.

Some everyday abilities that people around you may display, one of which you might like to model, are:
* how to pay or receive compliments
* making good decisions quickly
* capturing the essence of a book or a complex situation
* the ability to assemble flat-pack furniture
* sorting clutter
* stopping mind-chatter and becoming focused
* leadership skills.

If you want to model someone's skill, you want to know exactly how they go about it. This involves observing not just what they do and the order they do it in, you also need to know what they believe about it, what they are thinking as they are doing it and the things they say to themselves before, during and after doing it.

There are many practical applications for modelling. The trick is to learn new strategies which you can replicate and adapt, then use these new abilities to enhance your everyday life.

Modelling is a practical skill

When I felt twinges of RSI in my wrist, I decided to model the skills of someone who wrote equally well with both hands, so I could lessen the strain on my left arm. Finding an ambidextrous person who had acquired the skills in adulthood was difficult but also illuminating. James, an architect, had broken his right arm at university and taught himself to write fluently with his left hand in order to gain his degree.

I asked James to imagine the first time he had written automatically with his non-dominant hand and to re-enact the process. By modelling his behaviour and sensory processes around writing, I discovered that the quickest way to master hand control and writing legibly was from a standing position. The body weight should be evenly balanced on both legs to give a feeling of being grounded, and for poise and control of the pen. The writing surface should be at kitchen-surface level, or some convenient height to aid writing in an upright position.

I had never heard of such a writing strategy before, yet as I listened to James I was struck by how obvious it seemed. Interestingly, James had not been consciously aware, until now, of how he made his initial breakthrough or what his actual strategy had been.

Installing a new habit

I set my intention to spend six to ten minutes each morning for 30 days writing for either clarity, speed or flow. I maintain my new habit by spending two minutes a day writing to-do and shopping lists, while standing up. Within a month I could write fluently with either hand.

If you want to enhance your performance in any sphere then the best way to do this is to model the behaviour of the people around you who already possess these skills.
* What are the person's beliefs that support the skills?
* How does body language and demeanour change as a person recounts or runs their strategy?

* Don't ask people 'why' they do things, instead ask 'how' they do them. This is a clean way of questioning which does not impose on people's own model of the world. 'How' will elicit the person's process for how they do the task.

Eliciting a strategy

Ask the person to carry out or re-enact the behaviour imagining they are actually performing, rather than observing the task.

* Find out the very first thing the person is aware of as they enter the cycle of behaviour.
* Note which representation system they are using to enter the loop by listening for 'I see', 'I hear', 'I feel', 'I need to'. This will tell you the initial state the person needs to be in to start the process.

If they need to be prompted, then ask:
* Did you see an image in your mind's eye?
* Did you say something to yourself like 'that's a job well done'?
* Did you have a feeling about it?
* Are you triggered by something internal or external? Do you here an inner voice, a memory or feeling?

Stringing the strategy together

Ask the person what they noticed next (picture, sound, feeling), and again identify the sensory representations. Keep asking the question, 'Was there anything you were aware of before that?' until the person's description of their strategy appears. Carry on until you get the complete sequence of thoughts, pictures, feelings and actions that the person runs to perform this task.

['Modelling Success Strategies', courtesy of *Positive Health* magazine (PH), Issue 120, February 2006, www.positivehealth.com
© Frances Coombes]

Janette Hurles, an advanced modeller, did a lot of research reading for work and wanted to find a way of distilling the essence of what was in the books. She chose three people to model who were excellent at this skill.

Through modelling these people she discovered that: 'They all thought systemically at a very basic level. They believed that all information was connected and part of a bigger picture.' Detachment and objectivity seemed to be key to all three people's strategies.

'If they are distilling information from a book, the people all hold the information in a map within their senses and they'll create a picture of the issue, and come up with a premise. So they'll think, "Okay, so this is what this is about."'

'One person said their picture was a "spider" with tentacles where different sorts of information was held. Another person said their picture was "Almost like a globe of the world". There were bits where they would say, "This fits into this and that into that". So as they're going through a meeting or book, what they're doing is looking for connections and relationships to their own internal model.'

Modelling requires you to take on the beliefs, physiology and strategies of another person performing a skill that you'd like to acquire. Start looking for people who display talents you admire and would like to have. Begin modelling by asking them, 'How do you do that?'

What to look for when modelling a skill

There are three things to look for when modelling someone's strategy.

* What are their beliefs that support the skill they are doing? Listen for words like 'I believe', 'I think', 'it's important that ...'. These words indicate that whatever they say

directly afterwards is important to that person and it is what they believe.
* Pay attention to how their body language and demeanour changes as they recount or run their strategy. Notice any change in their manner, posture and the way they hold themselves as they begin to relate their account and associate with the task.
* Notice at what point the strategy begins and ends. Once you have the person's strategy and know what makes them feel confident and competent about their abilities around it, you need to try on their beliefs.

Sit or stand as they did and adopt their body postures. Run through the strategy yourself saying it out loud as you perform it. Repeat whatever your model has shown and told you in precisely the same language they used. They will correct you if you're wrong because you have plucked this strategy from their world and the slightest mistake you make will jar with them.

At this point you have acquired the strategy. If you run it through and nothing happens for you, ask the person to do it again and talk it through because something may be missing.
* Listen and look for consistent patterns of behaviour.
* Pause to check out your insights.
* Relax, and then reach your conclusion.

Sometimes when people are so familiar with a process that it becomes a habit, there are parts of it that are so obvious to them that they fail to explain them. And the missing part is actually the most important piece of information that you need to make sense of how the strategy works.

Run through the strategy several times until you know you've got it and then practise using it over a few days. Decide whether the beliefs that this person holds around their strategy fit well with your own beliefs before deciding to adopt their strategy.

['Success Strategies', courtesy of *Positive Health* magazine (PH), Issue 120, February 2006, www.positivehealth.com
© Frances Coombes]

If you master modelling skills you will never be bored again. Each new person possesses hidden talents, and becomes the most fascinating person you could meet. It is your job to unwrap them and find their hidden talents as quickly as possible. Discover any skills they have that you do not yet possess but would like. Are any of their skills, interesting, challenging, awe inspiring, mind blowing? Then it is up to you to decide how you will model these skills and acquire them.

So get motivated – start increasing your modelling skills and taking the actions that make successes happen much more quickly.

10
coaching your inner team

Imagine you are team coach and about to choose your selection for the next World Cup. Which team members support you, and why will you keep them? What qualities do they possess that support your aims? Are there team members who don't support you? Will you get rid off them, and why?

Inside us we all have lots of inner team members, all have special qualities and want to keep us safe from harm, but some team members comments are unhelpful. Easy to recognize team members are listed below.

Do your inner critics tell you that you cannot do things? Are there members of your inner crew who need routing out and replacing with more supportive new team players? Is there an inner voice that says:

'I must be perfect.'

'I must please other people.'

'I must always hurry up.'

'I must be strong and not show emotions'?

Is your inner team working for you?

Inside us we have lots of different components that make up our inner team and contribute to the way we think. We might have a team member who says, 'I wake up each day and I feel good, and I expect good things to happen.' We may have another part of us who alerts us to things that are coming up in the future, who says, 'We must be prepared in case something unexpected happens.' We may have another team member who takes care of our welfare and says 'It's time we took a holiday.'

There may be other team members who, although trying to help us, actually undermine us. We may have parts of us that say, 'I can't do this' or 'I will never get it right', 'It's time for me to panic.' Their purpose is to help us and keep us safe and away from imminent failure, but the other function they unintentionally perform is to stop us reaching our full potential and being successful.

Your inner team strengthens or weakens self-confidence

Self-confidence relates to actions and how we view ourselves when we perform those actions. If we feel confident when facing an unfamiliar or difficult task we will expect to perform well. We review our memories of how we tackled new challenges in the past, and if we feel that we performed them well then we carry those confident feelings with us and expect that our success patterns will repeat themselves.

Sort out your inner team members

On a piece of paper, draw a line down the centre. Reflect on the thoughts and the things you most constantly say to yourself in work, testing experiences or difficult social/relationship situations.

On one side of the line, list the types of thoughts that support you and categorize them into which type of team member they are.

On the other side, list the members whose types of thinking do not support you, and give each one a name, for example:

Support	Team leader
I will do it!	Inner cheerleader
I am a good team member	Good supporter

Do not support	Team member
I will never do it	Inner critic
I can't get it right	Underminer

Who is working for you on your inner team?

Think back to situations when you did not do well. Write down the things you were saying to yourself about what was going on in your mind. List the things you said to yourself that supported you. List the things you said to yourself that undermined your confidence.

Look at your team and decide which members you want to keep, and which members you want to replace.

* Team members I will keep are my ...
* List of qualities each member brings that support me ...
* Team members I want to replace are my ...
* List of qualities that do not support me ...

Team members' intentions

All of your inner team members do the best they can for you, regardless of how helpful or unhelpful they are to you.

* List the team members you want to replace and, underneath each heading, write what you feel was the positive intention behind their undermining behaviour.
* List the new team members you want to replace them with, and the type of thinking that would support you and be more helpful to you.

Actively work to replace each unhelpful team member with another with the type of thinking that would bring about a positive change for you.

11
model success to master change

Few books have been written on modelling strategies, so I have included sections. The trick is not just to acquire the strategy; you have to install it in your behaviour patterns.

I collected 300 excellent strategies and, to test they worked, incorporated 30 of them into my own behaviour, with interesting and far-reaching results.

Combine and build the strategies you learn upon each other like cementing bricks when building a wall. Gather a few well-chosen tools and techniques from this book, and you can begin to generate your own unique strategies.

I am about to run new training sessions based on modelling Richard Gray's Brooklyn Programme, an exciting new substance abuse treatment programme, which uses NLP techniques we have covered. During the seven-year programme, a staggering 30 per cent of participants tested drug free on random urine analysis after one year.

Modelling is generative; who knows where your modelling strategies will take you?

Borrow other people's strategies

The simplest way to increase your skills is to pick an area in which you would like to improve, say, how to be a better home improvements person, computer user, parent, cook, lover, or how to develop better reasoning skills. Then find someone who has those skills and ask them 'How do you do that?'

How to increase your reasoning skills

Ask yourself lots of questions related to what you already know about the subject, and the things you would like to know. Write a list of your answers and, as you picture yourself using all your tools and techniques fluently, the images you picture will contain all the clues you need for acquiring skills patterns.

Self-questioning	Answers?
How do I reason now? What are the thinking through steps I take?	
How do I know when I have reached a conclusion? What are the signs that tell me? The feelings? The mind pictures? What do I say to myself that lets me know?	
How effective is my method of reasoning? Am I ever wrong?	
Do I sometimes have blindspots? If so, list what they are.	
Who do you know who excels at the skill you want to perfect?	
Could you watch them performing the skill in order to acquire it?	
Is there a simpler basic outline of the strategy that you could start with?	

Collect strategies to improve your situation

The trick is to keep a list of all the new strategies you have come across. You have so many tools to help you develop wider and more flexible reasoning skills. Which one will you pick?

Retrieving undisclosed information

Useful questions to ask are, 'How do you know that?', 'What are you assuming to come to that conclusion?', 'Do you have any evidence for what you are suggesting?' Reflect on whether the information you have been given adds up, and whether the opinion is justified or not. Ask yourself, 'What has come from the discussion that is new, different or moves the situation forwards?'

A frame for your questions

ASSUMPTION?	Listen to the people present and note what assumptions are being made.
EVIDENCE?	Are the points they are making facts or opinions? If points are put across as fact, what is the evidence for it?
ILLUSTRATIONS?	If a person gives examples of the points they are putting forward, are the illustrations consistent? If not, ask for a better example.
OPINION?	Based on the information they have put forward, is the opinion of the person making the statement justified?
UNIQUE?	Has any new information emerged? Are there any new key points? If so, separate out what is essential from what is padding.

You can employ the AEIOU reasoning strategy in:
* meetings, to gain clarity on a situation
* if you are anxious about how a decision is being made
* when you want to make changes
* if you are dissatisfied with a decision and don't know why
* if you are faced with a threat or challenge
* when you want to disagree.

Once this basic reasoning skill becomes a habit you will begin to use it every day. It will help you understand the most important points in what is going on. And, if you run your own ideas through the AEIOU questions before presenting them to others, you will understand the real objectives in a situation, be able to select an appropriate option and present your own findings logically.

Recipe for modelling a good decision-maker

Modelling a thinking style is like making a pizza. First you look in your techniques store and assemble the ingredients you will require to model the thinking style of a good decision-maker. A good decision-maker will always have:

* a framework for their questioning process, AEIOU questioning, will do to start
* flexible thinking, so that they can employ several different ways of retrieving information about a situation
* chunking up and down skills (big picture/small detail thinking).

Model the style of a good decision-maker

You can start to model good decision-making skills by watching television programmes that feature personalities who display the qualities you admire and wish to acquire. Television shows are excellent starting points for acquiring skills, as they stick to a regular format that lets you see the person perform the same process many times over.

Model how to develop good decision-making skills

The first time you watch a programme, refrain from getting drawn into the content of the discussion. Instead, take a pen and paper and look for the framework and patterns of behaviour that come across in the show. Note the questioning style the presenter uses to separate fact from irrelevancy. Discover how they tease out the most important information.

Choose a person who exhibits the skill

Shows featuring police procedure are good to watch for picking up thinking styles, provided you can ignore the story and stick with the procedure. Remember, you are watching to obtain a decision-making strategy. List what the subject is doing and noticing and paying attention to. You may already do this subconsciously, but writing a procedure down makes it explicit and lets you uncover strategies and recognize whether any parts are missing.

There is an American television judge who tries civil litigation cases in front of a television audience, and is incredibly good at sizing up a situation and then making a ruling based on her questioning process. This is what her framework, thinking style and process looks like when written down.

> **Eye accessing cues**
> She pays attention to eye accessing cues, and where defendants look to access information. You will hear her say, 'Look at me when you answer questions, don't look away.' She holds the belief that people who do not look her in the eye when giving information are probably lying.
>
> **Shifts in people's descriptive language**
> The judge notices shifts in people's language and viewpoint. Someone who is being questioned about what they were doing on the day the house was burgled may happily answer all questions: 'I went here'; 'I went there at this time'; 'I did this'; 'I did that.'
>
> However, when asked a direct question, such as, 'Did you steal the motorbike?', they may reply with: 'I would not do a thing like that.' This reply alerts her to the fact that they are probably lying. The person has shifted their viewpoint of the situation and is talking as if they are discussing someone else, from a distance.
>
> **Notice how people shift viewpoint as they speak**
> * **Position 1** is our own point of view. We discuss a situation as seen through our own eyes. We describe what we are feeling and describe our thoughts.
> * **Position 2** is from the other person's position. We put ourselves in their shoes and describe how they feel; we speak as if we were them. (Often when people tell lies, they feel uncomfortable doing it from position 1, their own viewpoint. So they may switch to position 2, distancing

themselves from the act and becoming an onlooker, giving a character reference for the behaviour being described.)
* **Position 3** is neutral. The situation is seen through the eyes of an impartial third-party observer looking on a situation in which the others are engaged. By changing our thinking to that of an onlooker, particularly in areas of conflict, we can gather vital information from a distance that people who stay engaged in the other two close-up thinking positions will miss.

Recipe for developing a good decision-making strategy
* Framework: always has a structure in which the questioning takes place.
* Questioning: to gather information.
* Chunks questions up and down: to gain different types of information.
* Models each litigant's thinking and behaviour: by asking each to run through everything they did and noticed.
* Notices eye accessing cues.
* Notices perceptual positions.
* Metaphors: makes comparisons of situations with similar circumstances which highlight anomalies in people's thinking and behaviour.

The above ingredients, and the judge's exquisite flexibility to move effortlessly through the different types of thinking and viewing situations, form the structure for how the judge's questioning works.

Good decision-makers develop analysis and problem-solving skills as well as good judgemental abilities. They take a step-by-step approach when sifting through evidence and are not distracted by emotional comments offered as if they are facts.

A decision-making framework
Start by obtaining the big picture
The judge uses flexible thinking steps as she tries a case. She puts the situation in a framework: 'Person A says this; Person B

says this. Here is my understanding of the situation.' She asks both plaintiff and defendant: 'How much of my understanding is correct?' Each question she asks follows a format, that guides the person's attention in a certain direction. What she is left with is two pictures, side by side, with some details the same and some which are different.

1 The judge uses chunking up by asking each person to describe a big picture view of the whole event.

Asks what happened and gets PLAINTIFF'S version of events. Asks, 'How much is correct?'	Asks what happened and gets DEFENDANT'S version of events. Asks, 'How much is correct?'
Looks for inconsistencies and what is different from defendant's version.	Looks for inconsistencies and what is different from plaintiff's version.

2 The judge then chunks down, saying 'Here are the sticking points' and moves to small detail–specific questioning. She asks 'Who?', 'What?', 'When?', 'Where?', 'Why?' and 'How?' questions to uncover inconsistencies.

Defendant:	They were in the car.
Judge:	Who's 'they'? Who else was there?
Defendant:	The guys in the car, who stole the video.
Judge:	How do you know they stole the video?

The Judge models each litigant's thinking and behaviour, as they run through what they did and noticed from before to after the incident. The questioning allows her to look for inconsistencies and relevant facts to back them up.

3 The judge then changes to position 3, impartial thinking. At this point she has the facts and moves to position 3, an impartial observer. From an impartial position she separates litigants' feelings from facts.

Feelings	Facts
'I know you are feeling bad sir, and looking for someone to blame.'	'But the fact is, your daughter ran off with this man. No one forced her. She went willingly.'

11 model success to master change

Often in heated situations people are illogical in what they are saying and thinking. It is always helpful to take a deep breath and separate what is fact from what is feelings to help reach an accurate conclusion.

4 **The judge summarizes the case and her conclusions** about participants' motives and the logic of their actions and offers her own reflections, such as, 'You weren't smart, to leave your key in the ignition and walk off', or, 'I'm curious to know what occurred within two days to make you give up your morals and take the money?'

5 **Take action.** Finally she makes a ruling and awards compensation to the injured party, or says, 'You both behaved badly. Pay for your own expenses.' And the case is over.

What a questioning framework does

If you use a questioning framework for your own decision-making it will allow you to:

* ask questions to clarify your motives
* give understanding on whether your objectives are clear
* explore whether all options have been identified
* quickly identify any areas in which you have been blinkered
* show steps left out from the thinking-through process
* know whether you have enough information to support your analysis.

What modelling someone else's effective strategy gives you

* The chance to see up close what makes someone excel at something they do well.
* The opportunity to acquire that ability in a fraction of the time it would normally take and make it your own.
* The chance to try on the beliefs, capabilities and behaviours that combine to make that person's strategy so powerful for them.
* The opportunity to try on a strategy immediately and identify what works and what does not work.